I0448938

LIFE'S JOURNEY OF AN IMMIGRANT

(A TRUE STORY)

Charles D. Chambers

authorHOUSE®

AuthorHouse™
1663 Liberty Drive
Bloomington, IN 47403
www.authorhouse.com
Phone: 1-800-839-8640

© 2010 Charles D. Chambers. All rights reserved.

No part of this book may be reproduced, stored in a retrieval system, or
transmitted by any means without the written permission of the author.

First published by AuthorHouse 3/18/2010

ISBN: 978-1-4490-9890-2 (e)
ISBN: 978-1-4490-9889-6 (sc)
ISBN: 978-1-4490-9888-9 (hc)

Library of Congress Control Number: 2010903483

Printed in the United States of America
Bloomington, Indiana

This book is printed on acid-free paper.

Edited by Kathy Pooler
Publications Plus
Norwich, Connecticut

FOREWORD

Charles D. Chambers (1920 -) was born in England and immigrated with his wife Dooly and three children in 1953 to the United States. The following is the story of his life in the U.S.A. from 1953 to 2009.

CONTENTS

CHAPTER ONE

On February 15, 1945 a USAAF B 25 Marauder took off from St. Mawgan Airfield in the UK headed for Base Air Depot No. 1 for modification tests and acceptance before being accepted and assigned to a USAAF Squadron. It carried a crew of two, Lieut. Kenneth Mace (Pilot) and Cpl. James Burser (air mechanic).

During the delivery flight, Lieut. Mace apparently lost his way, and the Marauder veered off course and headed in a northwesterly direction towards neutral Ireland. At 1840 hours the plane was observed by the Gardia in Camolin, Co. Wexford heading south and the pilot who did not know that he was over Irish territory, looked for a suitable place to land, but could not find one.

When the aircraft engines stopped, due to a shortage of gas, he was able to retract the undercarriage and was eventually able to crash land the aircraft in a field near the village of Killenagh, 6 miles south of Gorey Co. Wexford.

Neither of the occupants on the plane were injured, but the aircraft was badly damaged, and both airmen after leaving the plane, were escorted by the Gardia to the police station in Gorey.

At that time, I was in the RAF and stationed in the North of Ireland at a salvage unit in Glengormley, just outside Belfast. I had only been with this unit for a couple of months, having just returned from Iraq where I had been stationed for the last 3 years. My first assignment was to go down to the South with a salvage crew and pick up the wreckage of the Marauder and bring it back to the north.

Little did I know that this trip was to change the course of my whole life.

On the morning of February 16, myself and my crew arrived in Gorey and procured lodging in a small hotel called the Bridge Bar Hotel, which was situated at the far end of the main street. After getting settled in, we proceeded to the site of the wreckage to examine and plan our recovery of the badly damaged plane.

We then spent the next three days loading the wreckage on to low loader transports for transport back to the north. Although our days were mostly taken up with doing the job we were sent to do, our evenings in Gorey were generally spent in French's Pub on the main street, sampling the local brew, which of course was Guinness, which we did with much enthusiasm. We certainly found that the work we were doing gave us a terrible thirst, which Big Michael John French who ran the pub, catered to that thirst with due care and attention.

French's seemed to be a popular spot, I suppose being right in the center of the town and Michael John, a soft spoken friendly man, but not one I think you would want to cross words with, who seemed to be well liked.

I left the pub early that evening, and as I stood out on the sidewalk, I watched a group of men idly standing around on the corner beside a lamppost. They were just standing around watching the general run of pedestrians and traffic roll along the main street of Gorey. Just the usual small bunch of men with nothing to do but pass the time in idle chatter with the hope that something unusual would happen to brighten their day.

One man, who I afterwards found out they called, "the dutcher" (don't ask me why, only God and the Irish new that), seemed to be the comic of the group, and just as I stood and watched them, a very elegantly dressed older lady passed them leading a small dog on a leach. She stood and waited on the corner to cross the street and as she waited, the little dog who had been sniffing at the base of the lamppost, cocked one leg up and started to do his business. The lady, who obviously knew what her little dog was doing, stared vacantly about as though still waiting to cross the road, still clutching the leach in her hand. Although the dog had finished, she still continued to stand looking vacantly around, while the little dog who now stood on four legs, patiently waited for her to continue. After a couple of minutes of this the dutcher peeled his way from the group of men and slowly walked up behind her and gently tapped her on the shoulder.

"You can pull the chain now mam," said the dutcher, "your little dog has finished." The lady, in much confusion, moved on with her little dog following behind her.

At that time in 1945, Gorey was a small country town with only about four hundred families living in it, by all accounts mostly related, it was said that you should be careful who you call names, you may be naming the whole town.

Generally speaking, especially in small country towns like Gorey, it was not considered proper for women to drink in pubs. The only exception was a small backroom at the end of the bar, with the door always closed. This particular evening, old women would come in the back door and have an occasional "nip" so to speak. It was a little private room and was called "the snug." This particular evening, a friend that I had met who had been sent down from the Irish Air Corp to assist us whose name was Sean Dawler, was sitting at the bar with me, and I asked Big Michael if he knew of any young ladies who would like the company of two lonely airmen for a little chat and relaxation. We assured Michael that our intentions were honorable and that we would meet them in the snug at the back of the bar. We'd be very grateful. Michael was very helpful and said he was sure that he could get a couple of girls that would be only too happy to meet any of the airmen who had anything do to do with the crash.

Incidentally, the plane crashing so close to Gorey had become quite a source of excitement, and it wasn't surprising that anyone in the town would be delighted to meet anyone who had anything to do with the crash.

Anyway, the two girls that we eventually met were sisters, Eileen and Louie Redmond, daughters of the local butcher and farmer, whose shop, "the blue house" was directly opposite French's, on the main street, and who happened also to be related to Michael John.

We both came into the pub at about 9 o'clock and proceeded to the snug where we found the two girls waiting. Sean went in first and sat beside Eileen, and I followed behind and sat down beside Louie. We had a very pleasant time with the two girls and after a few drinks, I suggested we walk down to the Bridge Bar where we were living and I would show them some of the small pieces that I had collected from the wrecked plane.

The Bridge Bar lay at the end of the main street, only about ¼ mile from French's, so we walked down to it and went into the main bar of the establishment which was pretty well empty.

I ordered some drinks from the bartender and we all sat down at a table and after a few minutes I got up and left to get the few pieces that I had of the wreck and bring them back to show the girls. When I returned, I found the two girls and Sean standing ready to leave, while a very irate older lady, who was the owner of the pub, letting them know in no uncertain terms, that, "she had no intentions of allowing young or old ladies drink in her establishment, and would they please leave immediately."

The women would not even let us finish our drinks, but practically drove us out. It would not be the last time I would run foul of the local customs in small Irish villages at that time.

But I think I understood, and learned to respect their wishes and their ways more and more as the years went by. Far from that one incident of unhospitality I always found the Irish to be kind and generous and hospitable in so many ways, and I never felt that they looked or treated me as a "stranger" in their country.

For the time of the year, I remember the evening while chilly, was really very pleasant. Maybe it was the company that we were with, for I suddenly felt my heart going out to this Irish Colleen. The girls took us back to their house which was on John Street, which was a small street just off Main Street.

We sat together in a small cozy living room beside a friendly open fireplace, and Eileen cooked us up an Irish "fry" and made us tea. I never really had a fry before. It consisted of slabs of bacon, sausages, black sausage, white sausage, brown wheat bread and eggs together with good hot strong tea.

We sat and talked and laughed and got to know each other until 1:00 in the morning. I think I would have stayed until dawn, except Mr. Redmond, Louie's father, who slept above the living room hadn't pounded on the floor with his stick, and told us to stop making so much noise.

We left Louie's house, and I arranged to meet her the next day before I left for the North, although I'm happy to say that when we got back to our lodging, I found a note saying that we would not be returning to the North for a few more days.

I woke up early the next day, and in a way, it being a free day, with our work on the crash site completed, I decided to take a walk around the small Irish town, for somehow I wanted to know it better.

I found that pretty well all people I met on the street as I walked around, were friendly and greeted me with a smile and a touch of the hat, as though I was another neighbor. I went into many of the shops on the main street and was very surprised that even on some of the smaller sweet shops, and bakeries, they all had a little bar where they would sell you a bottle of Guinness or beer, or a shot of Irish whiskey. It seemed that in those days practically anyone if they owned a business of any kind, could get a license to sell beer and spirits.

Many years later, as I write this, it is now practically impossible to get a license through the Irish government.

There are so many licenses out and around, that the only way to get one, is to buy one from someone who already owns one and is prepared to sell it (at a price). The Irish, I have found, have a capacity for alcohol, second to none. Pubs are a way of life to them, a meeting place, a place for a bit of "crack," (fun) a place to do business to name a few. Most Irishmen have their own special pub that they will go to year after year. I've known many that would "give up" drinking meaning they would only drink Guinness or not touch the hard stuff. I have only known one Irishman who has never touched alcohol of any kind in his 66 years in Ireland. I won't mention his name, but he is a man I'm very fond of and have a lot of affection for.

One evening, I was sitting in French's talking to big John about this very subject, and he told me the story of just how far an Irishman will go to get a drink (legally). Mickey Doyle loved his drink and would get up early in the morning to be ready when the pubs opened at 8:00 a.m. But some mornings Mickey couldn't wait until 8:00 and although he would usually have an emergency bottle ready, somehow that bottle would get drank, and poor Mickey would be without until the pubs opened at 8:00. Then Mickey found a solution to his dilemma. If he got up at 5:30, and got on the 6:00 train to Dublin, the Dublin train had a bar on it, which was always open. He could then drink all he wanted for the hour than the train took to get to Dublin, then take the 7:30 back to Gorey, and drink for another hour to be back in Gorey where all the pubs would be open. Having been able to drink all he wanted for his 2-hour train ride.

When it came to having a drink, the Irish had so many ways of getting what they wanted.

The only day of the week that the pubs were closed was on Sunday, so that day you couldn't get a drink – right? No wrong!! You see, they had what they called the bona fides law in the South of Ireland, which meant that if you were a traveler, as long as you traveled one mile or more from your place of residence, you could enter a pub and drink legally.

So every Sunday, you could see all the men riding their bicycles to a pub that was at least one mile from their home, and they could drink all they wanted.

I never did watch to see them coming home, by God! That must have been a real sight to see.

Before going back to the North, I asked Louie Redmond to marry me, and although it took her a long time to say yes, (at least 5 seconds), I knew that she loved me just as I loved her. Being the English gentleman that I thought I was, I asked her father and mother to be sure that they had no objections.

The mother appeared a little apprehensive at first, but I found out later that it was not against me. She was not afraid that I would make her daughter happy, but that her daughter would make me happy. Time was to prove her very wrong.

Having a few days before going back to the North, Louie brought me around to meet many of her friends and relatives, and they all accepted me as a member of the family although we were only verbally engaged.

Louie came from a large family with three brothers and three sisters, Mollie, Eileen and Margy. Mollie lived in Wexford, and I remember we went up to see them where I met Nial, who at that time was 4 years old and couldn't say Auntie Louie, but called her Auntie Dooly.

I somehow cottoned on to that name, and she has been Dooly to me ever since (if I ever call her Louie she gets mad at me and wants to know what is wrong).

One day we went to visit an elderly relative of hers who lived in Wexford. An ex-nun who had retired and lived alone in a very handsome home but had many friends and relatives who lived around her. She had a very broad Irish accent, and at times when she was talking to me, I found it very hard to understand her. She served up a beautiful meal, and was a very hospitable hostess in every way. At the end of the meal, she asked me if I would like some dessert and offered me some apple pie. Having eaten my fill to nearly a point of bursting, I declined and she exclaimed in surprise, "are you afraid it will make you faart." Without thinking I completely misunderstood her and although somewhat surprised, I thought she had said, "are you afraid it will make you fart." She had of course said fat, but with her broad accent on the "a", I thought she said something else. Not to hurt her feelings, I answered back and said, "OK I'll have some apple pie and take my chances on passing wind. Well, the poor ex-nun threw up her hands in dismay and looked me in the eye and practically screamed at me, "Oh you bold boy, you'll get no tay (tea) for that." But I did, although I tried to apologize to her and tried to explain, but I don't think she really got over it all evening.

When I returned to the North after our job was completed, I put in for leave which I had coming, for I had arranged with Dooly to come back down South and have more time with her so that we could get to know one another better before we got married. I doubt if we had spent much more than 12 hours all together in the short time that we had known each other. Before I could go on leave, my C.O. informed me that I had to go over to London, England where a technical course had been booked for me in my name. I would only be gone a few weeks and then could go on the leave I was looking forward to, down South.

Calling Dooly on the phone, I explained the situation and told her I would call her when I got situated in London. When I arrived in London, I found it a mad house, the war was going extremely well for the allies, and people had been traveling to London, by the thousands, the place was packed, and it seemed that celebrations were everywhere. The place where I was booked to stay was jam packed, and I found that I had no accommodations. I scoured the area for lodging to no avail. I ended up sleeping on a park bench in Hyde Park for the next few days, and my communication to Dooly to please her seemed at the time, a minor problem compared to my present situation.

When I tried on public phones to get through to Gorey, I found that the lines were blocked, so I sat down one day and wrote a note to Dooly to let her know that I still loved her and would contact her as soon as I was able. Well eventually I returned to the lodging that had been booked for me, and they managed to take me in. The course that I was supposed to take had been cancelled, and after making arrangements to go back to Ireland, I returned to my lodging to find a very irate letter from Dooly in which she told me in no uncertain terms how she felt that a man would tell her he loved her, ask her to marry him, and then just disappear without a word. She reminded me that I had promised to phone her as soon as I arrived in London. I did finally get through to Dooly by phone, and found a very contrite and tearful Dooly who had gotten my letter (they must have crossed going over the sea) and assured me that she didn't mean anything that she had said in her letter and please come back to her as soon as possible. As soon as I returned to my unit in Glengormley, I applied and was granted two weeks leave, and changing into civilian clothes, I packed and was on the way to the railroad station to catch the train for Dublin. I had phoned Dooly before I left, and she had promised to meet me in Dublin, and then we would take the bus down to Gorey together.

If you've never taken a bus in Ireland traveled down the country roads, stopping at each stop to take on and let off passengers, I wouldn't recommend it if you have no stomach for hospitality and alcohol. Somehow the bus drive to Gorey evolved into a country drive of friends and relatives who we picked up and dropped off on every stop on the way down. Each stop that we made just happened to be the local pub of the little town or village that we stopped at. This was an excuse for everyone on the single-decker bus, including the driver and conductor, to get off the bus, stretch their legs, and of course have the usual refreshments. By the time we were halfway to Gorey, I was feeling no pain. I'd never been a heavy drinker but when you are drinking with the Irish, you'd better watch your step.

By the time we came to Gorey, I had made more friends that I'd had in a lifetime, and have a hazy recollection of all of them. As we drove up the main street, I noticed this huge crowd that was milling around Jimmy 64 Pub, which was our stop. I thought that there must be some kind of a fete or something going on in the town to warrant such a crowd that was mulling around the bus as it came to a stop. Little did I know that I was the fete. Gorey had got the impression that I was the Marauder pilot that had come down with the crashed plane and that Louie was engaged to him.

As I stepped off the bus, having been the recipient of the hospitality of the Irish, I fell flat on my face, and lay like an idiot, with my nose flat on the sidewalk. As I got very unsteadily to my feet, I heard a voice in the crowd say, "Be Jesus he's no American, he must be one of us." And I've always felt to be "one of us" by the Irish to this day.

CHAPTER TWO

Although I was born in England, I have not lived a total of more than 5 years in that country in my life. My father was a career officer in the British Army, and practically from the time of my birth through all of my childhood and teenage years, we had traveled and lived all over the world including India, Ceylon, Germany and many other countries.

Being in the R.A.F., I had just returned from Iraq, where I had spent the last three and a half years, stationed just outside Baghdad in a place called Habaniya in the desert. When the second World War broke out, I decided to join the R.A.F. in the engineering division, rather than the army, which my father would have preferred. My parents were not religious people, although I suppose that I had some hazy beliefs in

God, but as was usual with most Englishmen at that time, I called myself a C of E (Church of England) but had no religion to speak of. As to any knowledge that I may have had of the R.C. Church, it was generated more by the atmosphere that surrounded it in the North of Ireland at that time.

When I came down to the South of Ireland to pick up the wrecked airplane, it was my first visit to that country and I must confess I was very impressed with the faith that the Irish people seem to have in their religion. But not having been indoctrinated into the Catholic Church as a child during my formative years, I was able to take a more dispassionate view, and really had accepted what I saw without too much thought. It came then as very much of a surprise when Dooly informed me that she would have to obtain a dispensation from the Catholic Church before she could marry me because I was a non catholic. It was also necessary that I sign some documents saying that if and when we had children, that they must be brought up and educated in the Roman Catholic faith.

This didn't bother me that much, but I did feel that the church was being a little heavy handed in their approach, and felt a little like they expected me to marry the Catholic faith as well as Dooly. Signing to say that I would educate and bring up the children as Catholics was something else, but I felt at the time that I would cross that bridge when we had to cross it (no pun intended).

So we both trotted down to the local parish priest, a vinegary old man, by the name of Canon Harper, and were duly ushered into his presence.

When Dooly explained to him the reason for our visit, I could feel the hostility that was building up. He told me that he did not want me there while he listened to the "problem" as he put it, and would talk to Dooly alone.

I left the room and waited outside, and although I couldn't make out what was said, the conversation was becoming louder and I knew a big argument was going on between Dooly and the priest. Finally, the door opened and Dooly looking very mad, grabbed me by the arm and said, "Let's get out of here. I'll tell you when we get home."

Dooly said nothing as we walked home, but I could see that Irish temper boiling up inside her. I said nothing, feeling that it was better for us to get to her house, where we could sit down calmly and discuss whatever the problem was.

When we got home to her house, she sat down in front of me and told me that the first thing the priest had said was, "Why was it she was wanting to marry a man who was not only not a Catholic, but an Englishman as well. Wasn't there some nice Irish lad in the town that would do her just as well?"

Well that set Dooly off until the priest said, "What's the matter, are you that way." Meaning was she pregnant.

Well that's when Dooly really lost it. She yelled back at him, "No I'm not, but if it will help things along, he's waiting outside and we can do the job right away."

The interview ended, but before leaving she insisted that the priest make an appointment for her with the Bishop so that she could plead her case with him.

Canon Harper was adamant that he would not under any circumstances grant her a dispensation to marry me. Yet when you think about it, he had never spoken one word to me, and yet had rejected me on the only fact that I was not a Catholic and an Englishman.

An appointment was made with the Bishop of Ferns in Wexford town, and a few days later we went up to see him.

Mrs. Kelly, who was Mollie's mother-in-law came up with us. A very devout Catholic, who liked her occasional glass of whiskey, for medicinal purposes only, as she put it, but a nice lady who I think wanted to come with us with the thought of meeting a Bishop.

As we were ushered into his presence by a young priest, the Bishop greeted us very cordially and asked us all to sit down so that we cold discuss the situation,

Before we got started, one of the housekeepers entered the room carrying a large silver tray on which was a bottle of Irish whiskey, a bottle of port wine and four glasses. He asked us if we would like a drink, and we said we would except Mrs. Kelly, who clutched her hands in prayer before her, looked up and into heaven and with very pious voice said, "Not for me your worship. I never touch the stuff." Well I'll be!

I thought at the time that maybe this religion had something going for it, although never having met an English Bishop, it seems this is not the treatment you could expect from them. I always tell people this story and add with my tongue in my cheek, that this was the reason I became a Catholic.

The Bishop seemed a very kindly man but Dooly's pleas were to no avail. He would not give her the dispensation to marry me. He had all kinds of Catholic and religious reasons for refusing us, but the answer was still no.

Dooly insisted on seeing some higher authority and after much thought and discussion he explained that the only one she could go to was the Apostolic Nuncio, the representative of the Pope who resided in Dublin. This was the higher Roman Catholic authority in all of Ireland. He would see what he could do to make an appointment and would let Dooly know. It seemed to me at the time that it was not normal for the average person to see the Apostolic Nuncio, that this generally was reserved for those that had the power and money to do so. I had to return to my unit and therefore when the appointment date came due, Dooly had to go up by herself.

Dooly's family was a well known old Irish family and were quite wealthy. There support of the Church financially, I'm sure, was pretty extensive, and I've always felt that her brother Paddy brought some pressure on the church to get the dispensation. Dooly never did tell me what happened in Dublin, but she did say that the A.N. walked her back across Phoenix Park where his palace was and told her, "Not to worry her pretty little head, she would get her dispensation."

I decided to take the bus back to Dublin, where I would catch a train to go back to the North of Ireland. When I left Dooly, and although at that time she was still waiting for her appointment with the Apostolic Nuncia, she didn't seem too worried and assured me that regardless of the outcome of her meeting, she would still marry me, even if I had to be in a registry office.

I had the option of taking the train from Gorey to Dublin but I really had enjoyed the bus ride down, and I would have company on the way back, for an Aunt of Dooly's who was down in Gorey on a visit from Dublin where she lived, was returning on the same bus.

Aunt Eileen was a nice lady a sister of Dooly's mother and I looked forward to traveling with her. The bus was about half full, and as I expected everyone was very friendly and seemed to know who I was and several asked me if I had got the dispensation yet. As very few people had phones in those days, the lines of communication amongst the people of the town of Wexford, which was the point of the buses departure and Dublin must have been something extraordinary.

The journey was uneventful until we had been on the road for about 20 minutes when we were driving on a very narrow country road with a field on one side and a small farmhouse or sheds on the other. Suddenly a gate from the field was opened and a herd of cows came pouring out in front of the bus. Behind the cows, the farmer with a short stick, was herding them over to the farmhouse for milking. Somehow we got tangled in the middle of the herd and the bus came to a halt with cows all around us. None of the animals were hurt, and didn't seem to be much put out by the presence of the bus. Suddenly one of the cows came a little to close to the side of the bus, and brushed against the side view mirror, breaking it off. The driver and conductor didn't seem too put out by this, but both got out to survey the damage. The farmer joined them after first seeing his cows safely in the farmhouse, and the three men stood around the broken mirror, discussing cattle, the price of cattle, the weather and how much the price of Guinness had gone up in the past few months.

Suddenly a young boy appeared with a roll of black tape and with plenty of verbal help from the three men, managed to stick the mirror back on, to which the driver replied, "that will do until we get back to Dublin, thanks be to God."

Quite what God had to do with it. I'm not to sure.

Everyone on the bus seemed to enjoy the whole escapade, with many suggestions thrown out as to how the mirror should be repaired. No one seemed to take very much notice of the suggestions, and it didn't seem that it was expected anyway, so we continued on our way, and everyone settled down to the rest of the journey.

I was dozing off beside Aunt Eileen when she suddenly shook me awake and told me that she had a problem. I woke up in a hurry, and somehow thought her problem had something to do with the cows, why I thought this I don't know, but as the only thing unusual that had happened was the cow incident, it just seemed logical. Well, it turned out it was nothing to do with the cows. Aunt Eileen very badly wanted to go to the toilet, and as we were some ways from our next stop, she felt she couldn't hold it. I called the conductor over and explained the situation. "No problem," he said, "we'll just stop the bus near one of the cottages, and I'll knock on the door and I'm sure they'll accommodate the lady, please God."

We were on a fairly sparsely populated country road at this time, but the bus pulled up at a small cottage beside the road. The conductor got out, went to the cottage door, knocked on the door and a youngish lady appeared and he obviously explained the situation to her. He came back to the bus, and told Aunt Eileen that everything was all right, that although they didn't have a toilet in the house, she had a chamber pot that she could use. Aunt Eileen got of the bus and went into the house.

When she returned after about 15 minutes, I asked her if everything was all right. She said that the lady had been very nice, but that after she had finished there was a basin of water left for her with soap and towels so she could wash up afterwards. But when she asked how she would dispose of the contents of the chamber pot, the lady told her not to worry she would take care of it. She said, "I have five children and am quite used to it, so be on your way, and God be with you."

Aunt Eileen said I tried to argue with her, but the woman wouldn't hear of it. Where in the world, would anything like that happen, except in Ireland.

Ireland is such a beautiful country, and having lived in so many parts of the world, I've always been aware of the beauty of the various kinds of terrain that existed around me. It is something you appreciate especially on a bus journey in Ireland. But Ireland seems to have something very special about it with its soft rolling hills, and its meandering brooks and streams. The different villages that we passed through seemed to fit right into the landscapes as though painted in by an artist. As if they had been there for all time, which I suppose some of them had.

I had been introduced to Jimmie Redmond, Louie's brother, who ran the butchers shop on the main street and we became very good friends. I got to know a lot about the Redmond family from Jimmie. Paddy Redmond, Dooly's older brother, really ran the whole show and I learned that he was one of the best known cattle dealers in all of Ireland. The land, shops and farms, all came under Paddies supervision with Mrs. Redmond, the mother, being the financial officer and investor of the whole business. James Redmond, the father unfortunately had grown so old and senile it had been necessary at that time to hand the reins over to Paddy years ago. The Redmond family had lived in Gorey it seems since the beginning of time. The butchers shop on the main street could be traced back as being in the family over 300 years, and businesses in Gorey all seemed to be owned by brothers, cousins, uncles and Redmond's, and even John Street, the street that Dooly lived on, was totally owned by the Redmond family.

Michael Redmond, who actually was the eldest son, had been hurt in a football accident when he was a teenager, and was the only member of the family who didn't work.

He was always known as, "Eckers," which was his nickname (again don't ask me how he got that name), and I met him very rarely. I never did get to know him at all, for he seemed to spend most of his time in his uncles hotel, Jimmie 64, where a continuance poker game went on. I met many members of the family during the short time that I was with Dooly before we married, and I found them very friendly and that friendship continued over the years.

Another Michael Redmond, a cousin of Dooly's, who I met and went out to his farm just outside Gorey, I remember well, friendly enough because of a tree that he had growing in the middle of one of this pasture fields. I think it was the most beautiful tree I think I had ever seen. It was a huge tree, standing about 30 feet tall and I would say about the same in diameter at its bottom edge. The bottom edge of the tree was perfectly trimmed all the way around and the tree itself stood like a huge beautiful mushroom in the middle of the field. I asked Michael how did he trim the tree so perfectly around the bottom, but he said he didn't. The cows used to use the tree as shade in the summer and would nip off the leaves and branches at their height under the tree. Thus not only left it perfectly trimmed at the bottom, but aided in its growth all around at the top which gave it its beautiful round shape.

As with many of the Irish men at that time, Michael was not married. Very few of them married young, and it seemed to be the custom for them to wait until middle age, when they would then take a wife, usually in an arranged marriage, to a younger girl in her twenties.

At one of the many meals that I ate with so many different relatives, I remember one in particular where we all sat around the table chatting and generally have a good time as I did on so many occasions. The conversation usually centered around Dooly and what a wonderful person she was, and how lucky I was to be marrying her. I answered very gently, that I agreed with them and that when I first met Dooly, "I knew a good thing when I saw one." Well the conversation suddenly stopped and everyone looked at me in a strange way. I felt that somehow I had said something wrong and then Dooly gently told me that when I had called her, "a good thing," in Irish terms that met an Irish girl who was quite different from the person that they knew that she was. Let's say a girl of ill repute, was a 'good thing' in local terms.

At the dinner table they had a large jug which contained buttermilk, and on coming down to the South of Ireland, I tasted it for the first time and just loved it.

It was out at the crash on the first day that we were there, and after some very strenuous work I became thirsty and looked around to see if we had brought any water. Having none available, I walked over to the farmhouse that was nearby and knocked on the door and asked the lady who opened it, if she could oblige me with a glass of water. She immediately asked me to step inside and sat me down at the kitchen table, told me to wait and she would bring me something. When she came back, she carried a large tray on which what I thought was a glass of milk, a small jug and some cut slices of home baked wheat bread, and raison soda bread. She sat the glass in front of me, together with a plate of the bread and as I picked up the milk and tasted it while it didn't taste like milk, it sure was delicious. I was tasting buttermilk for the first time and I loved it. A staple of the Irish diet, I believe that it is the liquid left over after the milk has been churned in the making of butter.

Just another example of the Irish hospitality that I was to experience as I visited the South of Ireland. I ran into many obstacles when it came to the Roman Catholic clergy though, even to the time when Dooly and I were finally married in Wexford town at the Immaculate Conception Church. We were not allowed to marry in the church, but at one of the side altars that ran down each side.

To add insult to injury, while the priest married us, he refused to sign the register and although I'm sure Dooly was hurt by it, it didn't really bother me, for I'm sure the poor priests were only doing what they thought was right in the light of their Gods eyes.

In those days, in going around and meeting different people, I once remarked to Dooly how poor some of the people were. She looked me in the eye and said, "Don't ever think that they are poor, they just don't have any money. They have a home of their own, they have food on the table, and plenty of love in their hearts, they try to live by the Golden Rule, and when you have that, you're the richest person in the world."

What a wonderful girl I had married. I was indeed lucky.

CHAPTER THREE

I looked over at Dooly as I sat reading the morning paper and sipping my breakfast tea. I read out an advertisement that had appeared in the paper that morning. It was an advertisement, or more like a plea from the Ford Motor Co., in the U.S.A., asking for qualified technicians and engineers to work in their plant in Chicago, Illinois, where they were manufacturing jet engines which were needed for the war that was taking place in Korea.

We had decided a couple of years back to leave England and had hoped to find a better life in Canada, and had settled in Toronto, where I worked for a Canadian aircraft manufacturer. I liked the work that I was doing, but after the hospitality and friendliness of the Irish, I found it hard to get used to the cold and sometimes hostile attitude that the Canadian Nationals seem to have towards all new-comers to their country. We were all treated as D.P.s (displaced persons) and the company that I worked for and the Nationals that I worked with seem to have the same attitude.

Being a Catholic didn't help, for the movement of the Orange Lodges in Canada was strong. Even to having one of their lodges on the premises of the place that I worked. It seemed that you could forget any promotion if you were Catholic. Tolerated but ignored.

I had tried in the past to immigrate to the U.S.A. while in England, but had failed because I could not produce anyone to sponsor me, so the ad I was reading that morning in February of 1953, interested me.

Apart from the job itself, the thought of living in Chicago excited me. Al Capone, Tammany Hall and the many other visions that I had, mostly drawn from the movies, that I'd seen in part all relating to Chicago.

Both Dooly and I had always somehow set our goal on eventually getting into the U.S.A., and I think in our minds, getting to Canada, was the first step into getting into that country.

After talking it over with Dooly, I decided to phone the number that was given in the ad, which proved to be the American Embassy in Toronto.

I was put through to an individual, who when I explained that I was answering the advertisement, only asked me two questions. Was I a Canadian National, and two, a rough outline of my qualifications.

After I had given him a rough outline of my qualifications and explained that no, I was not a Canadian National, but a British subject, he seemed ready to close the interview but I did manage to give him details of the work I was doing in the aircraft company that I presently worked for. He finished the interview and thanked me for my interest and that they would let me know by mail if they needed anything further.

I left the phone feeling somehow that not being a Canadian National, but a "D.P." had again meant that I could forget it.

It wasn't until 5 days later that my feeling changed drastically. I came home from work to find Dooly waiting with a letter in her hand, and a big smile on her beautiful face. The letter was from the American Embassy in which they stated that they were interested in my qualifications that I had talked about over the phone, and that would I come for a personal interview with a time and date which they mentioned. They required me to bring certain qualifying documents and my passport with me. Both Dooly and I were delighted, but the one question I needed to ask of them, was this only a temporary visit, but would I be eligible to become a citizen.

The interview that I had at the embassy went very well, and yes, if I fulfilled all requirements required to become a citizen that after 5 years I could apply. They could see no reason why this could not happen. Even if the Korean War ended, and the plant closed down during the 5 years period, as long as I remained in America and was gainfully employed, I could still apply for citizenship after 5 years.

They told me that I would get confirmation by mail, would have to undergo a medical examination, and would be given the necessary instructions with regard to transportation and where and when to travel and my passport stamped with the necessary visa to enter the U.S.A.

My wife and family could follow me when I had got settled and found accommodations for them.

On May 31, 1953, I entered the United States of America and the first words I heard from a smiling customs officer at the U.S.A. border after he had examined my passport was, "welcome to America sir." It made my heart feel good, for in a way, I felt that I had come home, and knew that when Dooly and the children arrived, they would be happy as well, and feel the same way.

The factory that I was to work in I found to be one of the largest plants under a single roof in the U.S. It employed about 30,000 people and because of its size was spread over I don't know how many acres. You didn't walk around the plant, but because of its floor area, which was enormous, there were conveyances like golf carts, and small narrow "roads" between different sections of manufacturing that you traveled upon.

I was lucky, for I was assigned to the Forge area where the castings were made which housed the various parts of the jet engines. This section was situated very close to the road outside and fairly near the entrance to the factory so that I only had a short distance from the parking lot to my area of work. My job was the examination, measuring and testing of the 'first piece' off the casting of the mold, to ensure that all of the castings from that mold produced were correct in every way.

I loved the work, and the people I worked with. They were helpful, friendly and for once, since leaving England, I felt like a human being again.

In the next 12 months, I somehow had mastered the work where I was able to figure out a way of not only doing my job faster, but more efficiently and thereby saving time and money. This did not go unnoticed by my supervisor, for before I knew it, he informed me that they wanted to promote me to a section supervisor, but that I would first have to attend the 100 hour Ford supervisory training school. I was of course delighted and amazed that after such a short time not only on the job but in America I would be given a promotion. But after thinking about the things that I had learned in the past few months I had been there, and getting to know some of the people that I worked with, I began to realize that the average American that I met didn't appear to be interested in the responsibility of supervision or management.

If the pay was to their liking, and the work something that appealed to them and they were happy doing it, that was enough for them.

I found none of my fellow workers jealous or envious of my promotions, only good wishes and some I think felt sorry for me. The fact that I would be responsible for other peoples work just didn't seem to appeal to them at all. And this, as the years went by, and I learned to love this country and the people in it, I found to be true, and unfortunately applied to many of the male population and was carried over into their private lives.

But I am getting carried away, for my first reaction was to get home and carry the good news to Dooly, for with the promotion would come a substantial increase in my salary, and both Dooly and I had already had plans ready if and when we had the money.

When I first arrived in the U.S. one of my major requirements was to get Dooly and my three children down with me as fast as possible. I looked around to rent accommodations, something that would not only give us a home, but a place that would be suitable for 3 boisterous young boys. I discarded the idea of renting an apartment and looked around for something with some open space and eventually found something quite by accident in a small town just outside Chicago in Harvey, Illinois.

I say by accident, because being an avid golfer, I was driving to where a friend had suggested a small 9-hole course in Harvey which they thought I would like. It was a lovely afternoon as I drove to the course and had a very pleasant round of golf, and during the round I noticed a trailer park which was situated nearby, but not the usual type of trailer park, this was different.

The trailer park was located in a large stretch of open field with a small stream running behind it. Instead of the trailers, which were all very large standing in close proximity to each other, they all seem to stand on a large lot like a house built on each one.

Each trailer stood on about a half-acre lot and I noticed the number of small children that were playing outside there in swings and sandboxes.

After I had finished my game, I drove over to the entrance of the park, where a salesman greeted me with a smile of anticipation.

I learned from him that the park had originally been built to accommodate houses and that sewers and water lines had been put in to each half-acre lot, but for some reason the houses had never been built.

After laying idle for a while, a house trailer manufacturer had got zoning permission to put in and sell, large two bedroom trailers on each lot, as they were sold.

I asked him if he had any vacancies in the park and he said that he did, that a family was moving out as they had bought a house, and that they had their trailer up for sale.

He took me around to see the trailer, and I was impressed with how well kept it was, and how ideal it would be for my little family, but I couldn't afford the price.

I talked to the owner of the trailer. He and his wife seemed like very nice people, and sitting talking to them in the trailer over a cup of coffee, they agreed to let me have the trailer for what money I could afford, with the balance to be paid off in monthly installments.

They needed to do some checking up on me, but I gave them a deposit check, and they said I could move in two weeks. To say I was delighted would be putting it mildly, for I was missing Dooly a lot, her and the children, and at last we'd be a family again together.

Although we loved living in that trailer, and had paid off the balance of what we owed, our main consideration was always a real house of our own.

Our need for a larger house had become more urgent, for while the room that we had in the trailer for Dooly and I and the three boys was adequate, our family had increased with the birth of Alanna, and was becoming a little overcrowded, but still a warm and loving home.

With this new promotion and the raise in pay, we immediately started looking around for a house and eventually found one through a real estate agent called Bobby Haycheck, who not only became a good friend but a good neighbor as well.

The house we bought in 1955 was in Lyons, Illinois, just outside Chicago, close to the Brookfield Zoo, two houses down from where Bobby and her husband Ed lived as well.

My new promotion at Ford carried me further and I became part of a team of an engineering group of one of many engineering groups that were located in this huge factory.

In a way, at first it was a strange situation that I found myself in, for before I could enter into the office group that I would be working with, I first had to get a full security clearance through the U.S. Government.

This took about 2 months before I finally got this clearance, and in the meantime, although I was given the assignment and work necessary to do my job, I was not allowed into the office group itself, and was given a desk just outside the office door where I worked until the clearance came through.

The strange part was, that when I finally was allowed to go into the office after getting the clearance, I found the work I was given no different than what I had been doing at my desk outside.

But the U.S. Government is very thorough and my parents had written to me from England to inform me that the U.S. F.B.I. in England had not only questioned them at the house, but inquired of many of the neighbors as to my background and character.

I really loved that job at Ford, it was not only interesting, but the work atmosphere and conditions were great and the people I worked with so different to the people in Canada and England.

I found that all people I worked with, including my supervisors were on a first name basis. Yes, there was still respect for them, not the fawning, "yes sir, no sir" respect, that was so prevalent in the class system that I still found in Canada which incidentally I never found in Ireland. But a respect based on the man himself and the job he had to do.

One of the many things that I learned to love about America, was that all men were created equal, and you weren't looked down on, because you worked with your hands.

That regardless of your religious beliefs and where you came from, that the opportunities were there for you, if you were willing to work to get them and you were judged as a person, not because of your class or background. How could I not love this country.

Eventually, of course, the job at Ford came to an end with the war ending in Korea. I set out to find myself another job. Ford offered me a job in the car industry in Detroit, but

Dooly loved living in Lyons, she has always called it her home town, and after looking around at the job market in the area, I had no problem in finding another position in my field as a Quality Control Engineer.

Apart from the supervisory experience that I had gained at Ford, I had enrolled in college courses at I.I.T. in Chicago and had been studying at night with the hope of getting my degree.

The job that I had taken after leaving Ford was as a Q.C. Engineer, working under a man who was to change the course of my whole working life.

Harry Calder was a man who I learned was an extremely ambitious man. He had taken the job as manager of the plant, only as a fill in, for his sights were aimed higher. One of the jobs that he knew was available was with a company called G.M. Labs (no affiliation with GM Motors) for a manager to head up their Quality Assurance Department. I became quite friendly with Harry and he told me that although he had no problem with my work, he felt that I was under employed and that I should be working in a managerial position.

He suggested that I apply for the manager position at G.M. Labs, and that he would give me a letter of recommendation.

Feeling just a little nervous, I phoned up the company and made an appointment to go down to see them so that I could be interviewed for the job.

After being interviewed by a man with a heavy German (who I later found out to be part owner of the company) he told me that I could have the job and when could I start. I asked him what the salary would be and he said they would start off at $8,000 per year, and see how I progressed after that.

In 1960, $8,000 a year to me was a princely sum, and to go home to my family to inform them of my managerial position and the salary I would be making was a proud moment in both our lives. It could only happen in America.

For what we had accomplished in 7 years, and I say "we", for without Dooly's love and support I don't think it would have happened. To me it was a miracle.

We had a lovely house, a really good paying job, had made nice friends and had good neighbors, and to top it all, Dooly gave birth to another son in 1961, Rob. We were just one big happy family, and felt so lucky that we had come to America.

We really felt part of being an American, so because we both had lived in this country for at least the 5 years necessary to become citizens, we made out the necessary application papers and applied. And thereby hangs a tail which I often relate to many people.

After going through all the necessary paperwork and investigation we finally found ourselves in front of a judge with our right hand raised to be sworn in as citizens. The judge read out all of the requirements that we had to swear to, including one that stated that we would have to bare arms and defend America against any foreign power in the world, and would go to war against them if necessary.

Dooly and I were just two of about 20 people standing with our right hand raised, when he made this announcement, and as he finished everyone in union said, "I do," except Dooly.

In a loud voice in the quiet of the room, she said, "Your honor, I'll fight against all countries, but I won't fight against Ireland."

The poor judge looked at her with his mouth open, and I could see he just didn't know how to deal with this situation. He looked to the clerk who stood beside him and whispered something to him, and after examining a list, the clerk whispered something back.

"Margaret" the judge said at last, "I never heard what you said, but I can assure you that the thought of America going to war against Ireland is so remote that it isn't even worth thinking about."

Dooly and I became citizens that day, and Dooly has loved America ever since, just as much as I do.

Lyons was a great place to live and as a family we seemed to fit in extremely well.

It was very much a Catholic district, and the boys went to the local Catholic school which was run by a group of nuns.

I became a member of the Lions Club of Lyones, Illinois and enjoyed the comradely and fun that went with it together with the good work that the Lions did as an organization does, in its charitable works.

The events that were happening in my work carried me further along the line of progress, and although in all honesty I was content with what I had made of my life, more than content, circumstances seem to push me even forward, and I was offered a job in an industry that I was to stay in for the rest of my working life, at a salary that I couldn't turn down. The aerosol valve industry, and Aerosol Research and Development.

But I was able to pass on some of my own good fortune to someone who had been good to me when I first came down to the job in Chicago.

Joe DePetro was the superintendent of the large division at Ford, and when I first met him he inquired as to how I was doing and to turn to him if I needed anything.

By the time I had brought Dooly and the family down from Canada, and paid the down payment on the trailer, money by that time was pretty tight.

Television at that time was relatively new, and with the children clamoring for one, I tried to buy one on time with a small down payment, but was refused because of the short time that I had been on the job and in the U.S.A.

Joe got to hear of this from one of my co-workers and immediately called me into his office and told me what he had heard about the TV, gave me an address of a TV shop and told me they would let me have one on time, for a small down payment. I afterwards found that Joe had co-signed himself for the TV and being a newcomer and a stranger it was such a nice gesture, that I never forgot it.

Joe had stayed on at Ford for quite a while after they stopped production where he was needed to help clear things up.

When I left G.M. Labs, I knew that Joe had left Ford and had been looking for a job for some time.

I called up Joe and asked him if he would be interested in taking over my job, if so I would recommend him to my boss and I was sure they would hire him.

The rest is history, for although Joe was a lot older than myself, he got the job, and to my knowledge he worked for G.M. Labs until he retired at 65. I know that they were very happy with him as I knew they would be, for Joe DePetro was a good man.

Aerosol Research and Development (ARD) was a private company which had licenses in Bridgeport, Connecticut and in Portsmouth in the U.K. and was owned and operated by one Stanley Steinburg, who was my immediate boss.

Stanley was a man I never could figure out, and although he never really gave me much trouble in the three years I worked for him, for I did a good job for him and he knew it, his handling of the other managers and supervisors in the company left a lot to be desired.

We had a Plant Manager, two floor supervisors, a Production Manger and two sales executives when I arrived.

In the three years that I was there, he fired and rehired three Plant Managers, replaced the floor supervisor four times and fired both sales execs and hired new ones. How the production and sales department kept going, I'll never know.

He would get worked up in his office and you could hear him yelling a mile off.

I remember one time I was in his office during one of his many meetings of all his managers and supervisors, and he would be screaming and yelling with his face red and ready to burst.

I didn't know why, but his wife always seemed to call him on the phone during one of his tantrums. But the phone would ring, and when he heard his wife's name he would suddenly drop the rage and anger, be very normal with his, "Yes dear, of course my darling, etc."

Then his conversation with his wife would end, and as soon as he put down the phone, his face would redden, spit would appear at the corner of his mouth and he would continue his tirade, as if the phone call had never happened. The man was a maniac.

After talking it over with Dooly, I decided to quit ARD and as we had often talked of taking a holiday to England and Ireland, we decided to sell the house in Lyons and go back to England for an extended visit.

Whatever length of time we would be away, we both knew that we were not leaving America for good, for at that time, we knew that if we stayed away from the U.S.A. for longer than two years, in the land of our birth, we would lose our citizenship. We would never want to do that.

After much discussion with Dooly, we decided to go to the Portsmouth area where a licensee of ARD was located.

So in 1966, we set sail from New York harbor on a German liner, the Oceanic, to start a new period of our life together as a family.

CHAPTER FOUR

The ship that we traveled to England on, was a German luxury liner, The Oceanic that was returning to its home port in Germany after cruising the Caribbean's for about 6 months.

We embarked in New York and the ship sailed first to Cork Ireland, where it stayed for a couple of days letting off some passengers, then continued on to Southhampton in England where we disembarked and continued our journey by rail to Portsmouth.

The ship was practically empty of passengers, and we were very well treated by a crew that were all happy at the thought of returning home after being away at sea for so long.

My only complaint was the P.A. system, that used to pump out messages in German, with the first words flung over the loud speakers on the boat to announce that a message was forth coming. "Ach Tung, Ach Tung," it would bellow, then the message.

I felt we were on a German submarine at times, and that war was being declared again, but apart from that one annoyance, we all really had a very nice relaxing time with the food and service excellent.

Poor Dougie, who was in his early teens, during the skinhead era, had decided, unbeknownst to Dooly and myself, to be a skinhead and had shaved his head bald just before we left America. After seeing how ridiculous he looked, he obtained from somewhere a hat, like an old-fashioned trilby hat, and wore it continually and would not take it off. Poor lad. We sympathized with him, but nothing we did or said could console him.

After selling the house in Lyon, I was lucky to sell it for a lot more than I paid initially for it and had placed the proceeds in C.D.s with a Savings and Loan Bank in Chicago.

Having made all the arrangements well before we sailed, imagine our horror when the Savings and Loan Bank went belly up and we found all of our wealth tied up until the F.D.I.C. was able to reimburse us with our money.

We were lucky, for two days before we were due to sail we received a check for the full amount (less interest for the previous month), so we left America much happier, than we expected.

Somehow word had gotten to ARC in Portsmouth, England that I was returning and before I left the U.S. I received a telegram from England suggesting that I contact them when I had settled for they felt they could use my background in the aerosol valve business.

So it was with something of a light heart that both Dooly and I looked forward to a 2 year working holiday in England.

I had already made arrangements to rent a house in a seaside town just outside Portsmouth, but with the money we had, both Dooly and I had decided that if the job was right and we found a house to our liking, we would buy one, even if only for a short time.

I knew that having the cash, that if I saw something I liked, being a good bargainer, I'm sure I could come to a good deal, that when we eventually returned to the States, I could make a profit on it.

As I've gone through life I have always found that saying, "that money talks, and b.s. walks," has always been true.

When I contacted the company in Portsmouth I found them, after going through their small plant, and watching their manufacturing methods which were way behind the times, eager to offer me a job so that they could pick my brains, which had all of the high speed manufacturing methods that were used in the States at that time.

I told them that I wouldn't be staying more than two years, but that made no difference, so I was hired by their Managing Director and agreed to start as soon as I got settled.

A most peculiar man was Ronnie Reefer, the Managing Director.

At all his meetings that he held with his production and sales personnel, he would always have it in a large boardroom, always in the evening after work had stopped for the day, and always with a large bottle of Scotch whiskey at his elbow, which he drank quite liberally.

If you cared to drink with him during the meeting he had no objection, but although he slaked his own thirst quite often, it seemed to be understood by all present that you should not ask for more than one drink, even if he offered it to you.

Not being a drinker and disliking whisky, it never bothered me that much, except that on the evenings he had his meetings, it meant I never got home until late in the evening.

One of my first purchases was to buy a car, which I did and we were soon driving around the area looking at houses and taking in the scenery.

Portsmouth is actually a very interesting historical area and still is to some extent, one of the major ports of the British Navy.

Lord Admiral Nelson used Portsmouth in the old days as his homeport, and his wooden battleship the "Victory" is still tied up at the dock, or was when we were there and the public is allowed to go on the ship and see his cabin, and the rest of the ship and crews quarters.

One of the interesting features that I noticed about the living quarters of Nelson's cabin, was how small in height that men at that time must have been. The bunk that he slept in was so small in length, that it would hardly accommodate a boy much over 4 feet high.

We visited an old pub on the waterfront, called the "Still and West," where he used to meet with his officers to plan his battles.

There were many interesting places of interest, they all seem to have old pubs as their landmarks. One old pub called "The Bat and Ball" was a cricket club. Where cricket was supposed to have originated. Incidentally a game I could never take to for it could go on for weeks and always seemed to me to be most boring.

We did eventually come across a house which we really liked in an area called Inhurst Woods, and after much haggling and bargaining it became ours and in short order we moved in.

Inhurst Woods was a small area, set apart so to speak from the common herd, in which they had built about 30 homes, all of different designs, but to the English very modern and very upscale, all had central heating (something unheard of in England) all with large lots, and all owned by the more wealthier of the English, bank managers, solicitors and such like.

There's a saying that, "an Englishman's home is his castle" and believe me nothing is more true for when you live amongst them you soon find this out.

In the nearly two years that we lived in Inhurst Woods, I don't think I ever met any or said a word to even one of my neighbors, except one who had rented one of the houses a short distance from us, who turned out to be an American and his wife and two children and had been sent out by his company in the U.S. to help start up a subsidiary in the U.K.

I think if the English in that area had been allowed, they would have dug a moat around their castle, to make doubly sure no strangers entered.

I was never asked, nor did I ever visit any of the people's homes that I worked with.

Ronnie Reefer was never married, and the sales manager, a young man by the name of Roger Butcher, although friendly at times, seemed to feel in awe of me especially when he found out I had bought a house in Inhurst Woods.

When we left, David had wanted to stay in the U.S. and lived with Margie until we returned. Dougie hated England,

and eventually returned to the U.S, and joined the U.S. Army.

Terry stayed with us as of course did Alanna and Rob. St. Johns College in Southsea, was what they called in England "Public School" which in American terms was a private boarding school.

We enrolled Terry in that school and eventually Alanna in a private boarding school in a seaside town called Bournemouth where both of them stayed at their respective schools even when we returned to the U.S.

Both would eventually be going to university and after seeing the elementary education system in England at that time, we felt that a private school education would help them more when it came to going to college.

Living in Inhurst Woods was a nice experience, although the central heating system that we had in the house was not particularly efficient.

The hot water that was heated by a small coal stove in the kitchen and had to be continually fed with coal to keep the two or three radiators hot enough to warm the house.

While the house was well built, it had no insulation to keep the heat in. We finished up giving up on the central heating and did have a fireplace in the living room which kept us reasonably warm in the winter.

Our American friends down the road were luckier (or unluckier). The house that they were in was heated by electricity, coils I believe in the floor. The houses had no basements. When they first turned the heat on during their first winter, like any American they set the thermostat at a comfortable temperature and sat back and enjoyed the warm house, until they got the electricity bill.

Electricity in England is very expensive and the bill they got was equivalent to about ¼ of their total salary.

They appealed to the electric company to no avail. But I think they had a fireplace, and I don't think they used their electric heat anymore.

Although we were enjoying our stay in England, especially the many friends and relatives that came over from Ireland to visit with us, there were so many things about America that we missed, that when you live in the good old U.S.A. you tend to take them for granted.

Not being much of a drinker and certainly not a pub person, most Englishmen have their favorite pub and used it like a second home.

The few times I did go into pubs I found that it was the only time that I found a little humanity creeping into the rather aloof attitude of the average Englishman.

It seemed that it took a few pints of English ale to make them realize that somewhere inside that cold exterior there beats a heart.

We missed the warmth of the homes in the winter, the friendliness of neighbors, and above all the weather. Yes, it's cold in America in the winter where we lived in Illinois, but you expect the snow and cold, but it's a dry cold. Yes, the summers are hot, but you get to love the summers and the outdoor activities that are part of it.

The fall to me in America was the loveliest time of the year when the leaves on the trees displayed their colors and the air had that dry crisp feel, that smelled and felt so good.

Not to mention the spring. Four distinct seasons and each one unique in itself.

The weather in England for most of the year had only one thing that was constant, the damp and cold in the winter, and the rain and damp with occasional sun in the summer. It only ever felt like two seasons to me, winter and summer both damp.

The feeling in America that regardless of what you worked at that, you were judged by what you were as a man. In England I found the class system intolerable and was a little surprised that it still existed after so many years.

Part of the job that I was doing in Portsmouth meant a certain amount of travel over to Europe, to France and Germany and to the Channel Isles (Jersey).

On one occasion I had to visit Jersey where there were some plans to build another aerosol manufacturing facility on that island.

The owner and major shareholder of ARD in England was a wealthy man, who up to that time I had never met, who also owned a hotel where we would be staying in Jersey.

It was a large luxurious hotel and the man in question had private apartments on the top floor where he had lived most of the time.

When I was first introduced he addressed me as most Englishmen address those inferior in class to their own as "Chambers," not Mr. or my first name just "Chambers." I was expected to call him "Sir" but instead called him Mr. Latford which he passed off without incident but I could see he was a little annoyed.

That evening when I came into the dining room I was led to a small raised veranda overlooking the dining area in which were two tables set up ready for us to eat. This was his private dining area.

We were seated at our table, and in about 10 minutes Leonard Latford appeared with a young rather beautiful girl in her early twenties. Latford was a man in his late 50's, I was told later the girl was his mistress (girlfriend if you like).

Instead of sitting with us, he and the girl sat alone at the other table, waiters appeared and we all had dinner.

There was a small orchestra playing dance music and the people on the floor a couple of steps down from where we were, were dancing during courses.

As the only lady that was there at the table with Latford, I stood up and went over to her table and asked her if she cared to dance.

She looked at me without answering, and looked over at Latford and said to him, "Do you mind if I dance." Latford looked at her, said nothing to me, and answered, "I would prefer if you didn't."

I thanked the lady, who again said nothing to me and walked back to my table and joined the other two men who had come over with me. Just another example of the arrogance that the English showed, to anyone who they considered to be out of their class. Or maybe it was a way of putting me down because I didn't call him "Sir."

But I shouldn't dwell too much on the negatives, for in general Dooly and I, and the children enjoyed ourselves and were quite happy to have made the trip over to England.

In my travels over to France and Germany who were suppliers of some of the components for the valves we were manufacturing I found most of them friendly and very hospitable, especially the French who loved to entertain guests in some of their finer restaurants. I was introduced to some of their finer wines in the restaurant that they took me to and have ever since been a lover of good wines, which has been my favorite drink ever since.

The French have a relationship with their wines which I think must be second to none.

I had to take a train from Paris to Portia which is south of France, one cold winter day. The train left Paris at 12:00 midday and as was usual, I booked a table for lunch which was served in the dining car of the train.

At about 12:30 as the train was rolling along, I got up from my compartment and walked down to the dining car. When I arrived pretty well all the tables were taken, except one which the maitre'd led me to. As I walked between the tables to get to my chair, I noticed that most of the diners were sitting with what looked like bottles between their legs, as though they were trying to keep them warm. I asked the waiter what was going on and he told me in broken English that someone had left the window open of the carriage where all the wine was stored, and the temperature of the wine had chilled. The wine steward had ordered that lunch could not be served until the wine could be brought to a respectable temperature.

They had them pass out the wine in bottles to the diners, and asked them to warm up the bottle for them by placing them between their legs and covering the bottle with their hands.

It took about 30 minutes until the wine steward was satisfied, but as was expected, the lunch was delicious and the diners didn't appear to be put out by the experience.

In my experience, the English were not at that time great wine drinkers, except for Port wine, which I believe the more affluent kept and aged in their cellars.

The older and more aged, the better the wine developed.

I remember visiting one of our suppliers who manufactured the spring that is part of an aerosol valve. He was a kindly older man, and after we had conducted our business, he insisted that I join him for dinner that evening at his favorite pub where he said the food was excellent.

We had a very good meal and after we had finished he insisted that I have a glass of port wine, which he said was a specialty of the pub, because of its age. I agreed and eventually a waiter appeared wearing white gloves and a silver tray on which was a large bottle of port, a decanting vessel, and two wine glasses. The bottle was covered in dust and what looked like cobwebs, and after carefully removing the cork, the waiter first decanted the wine carefully into the decanting vessel and then just as carefully poured it into the wine glasses.

The old man watched the ritual with a slight smile and a look of anticipation as the waiter handed us our glasses.

The port wine was good, but not being a connoisseur of wine, I couldn't tell you how good, and the thought did cross my mind, that why not wipe the dust and debris off the bottle, before bringing it out. But that I suppose would have spoiled what proved to be quite an entertaining evening, and if it hadn't been for the dust and cobwebs, I may not have remembered the occasion.

England at this time had a tax system which was not only very high, but in some cases, a little hard to understand. Although I was paid a reasonable salary, which I had no quarrel with, the taxes that I paid took about 1/3 of my salary and in addition, because I owned my own house and had no mortgage, an amount equivalent to the value of the house which I would have paid in rent, was taxed as income, and I had to pay tax on money I didn't even earn or ever had. I believe after I left England this tax was canceled. But when we were there we had to pay it.

The car I bought had a 25% added tax, and pretty well everything you bought had a high tax added.

But these were things that we were aware of when we decided to leave the U.S., so they came as no surprise.

All in all Dooly and I were happy and enjoyed the time we spent in England. Dooly made friends with the American lady who lived in the area and seemed happy and content with her home and the children to look after.

We made some trips to London and spent some happy times at some of the many theatres and shows that were available. We visited Harrods, the big department store in Kensington, walked in Hyde Park, went to Buckingham Palace (no, the queen didn't ask us to tea) fed the pigeons in

Trafalgar Square and generally acted like tourists which is what we really were.

My job at A.R.D. had been going well and I was offered a permanent job as Plant Manager, but Dooly and I had already discussed plans as to our return to America.

The people that I worked with had become more friendly towards me, and our manufacturing had become more efficient and some of the manufacturing methods that I had implemented had been put into place, and I was happy to think that I had played some small part in the improvements that had been made.

I could see that Roger Butcher to a great extent was being groomed to take over from Ronnie Reefer as Managing Director, for Ronnie I knew would be retiring in a few years time, and even if I had stayed, which I had no intention of doing, my position with the company would have been limited.

The thought of staying and living in England for the rest of our lives, just didn't appeal to either Dooly or myself, and as the time drew nearer, when we knew that we had to leave, our resolve grew stronger as the months went by.

The company in Portsmouth had a fairly continual passage of communication with the factories in Bridgeport, Connecticut and the factory in Illinois and so it was no surprise to me when Phil Sagarin who owned the factory in Bridgeport, let me know that when I returned to the States that they had a job for me at his plant and would I consider it.

When I heard this, I immediately agreed to work for them, for I had met Phil Sagarin and had liked him.

A self made man who was a millionaire, and like all Americans, he was Phil to everyone. A man who loved to give parties for his staff, loved to sing songs at them and never touched alcohol of any kind.

So different from the English, for I was to remember an incident after I retuned to the States just a few weeks after I started work in Bridgeport.

Latford from England came over to Bridgeport on a visit and Phil Sagarin gave him quite a party to which all his managers and myself and our wives were invited.

During the course of the evening, Phil got up and gave a little speech in which he welcomed Latford, and afterwards Latford got up and gave a thank you speech in return.

Latford mentioned how much they appreciated what Bridgeport had done for them, but then to add that they should remember what they had done for Bridgeport. That they had given Bridgeport "Chambers." Not Charlie Chambers, not Mr. Chambers, but "Chambers."

I felt at the time like getting up and saying, "Hey Latford, my name is Charles D. Chambers, not Chambers," but I didn't. It would have put me in the same category as Latford and I was an American and proud of it. Not an underling.

In 1965, Dooly and I and Rob returned to the United States. We left Terry and Alanna in England to finish part of their education, which was their decision. Terry would be coming home next year to finish her high school education, and Alanna to stay to get her graduating educational levels.

If our stay in England for the short time that we stayed there, taught us anything, it taught us how much we should appreciate being Americans and being lucky enough to live in this wonderful country.

I have read many historical books about the war of an independence that was fought against the British in 1760, and the suffering that the Americans went through to gain the freedom that they have today.

The class structure that was of course much more rigid in those years, I still found traces of it that still existed while we were there.

An intolerance against anyone that was not white and born in the British Isles. An intolerance that I felt that they had towards the Irish, to the immigrants that had arrived form India and other countries that was apparent in the color of their skin.

I left England a little sadly, for somehow I had expected more from them than I got. Living in America had spoiled me, because I had been exposed to a culture which in many ways was so different to the one that we lived in for 20 months.

Someone once wrote, I don't remember the author, "Be there the man, with soul so dead, who never to himself hath said, this is my own, my native land."

As I said before, we enjoyed our visit, but my soul must be dead, for I have no wish to go back to England again, and I doubt if I ever will.

Chapter Five

In 1963, we returned to the U.S. and I started working for Phil Sagarin in his plant in Bridgeport, Connecticut. I liked working for Phil, who was a no nonsense man at work as I have already mentioned, but a man who liked to party although he was a strict teetotaler.

Although I had no title, I worked in a managerial position and was paid a good salary.

In addition to the salary, the company had a profit sharing system, by which they then added another ten percent to your salary and placed that into a fund which was managed by the financial controller and invested in the stock market.

After only being at A.R.C. Bridgeport for a few weeks, Phil asked me if I would go back over to France with their Chief

Engineer and check on some business that was necessary at that time.

The Chief Engineer, a man by the name of Bill Fauset, was a grumpy kind of an individual, a man about the same age as myself, who seemed to resent the fact that I had been chosen to go to France with him.

Over the years that I worked there, we eventually came to some kind of a truce, and although we never did get along to well, it never affected our working relationship, so it was something that didn't bother me.

The business that we had to attend to was in Paris, and we stayed at a small hotel off one of the side streets, the balcony's of our rooms was overlooking a small courtyard in the cobbled street.

Having been in France before, and also in Paris, I was very familiar with the comings and goings of the Parisians and their ways. Bill was not, everything was new to him.

During the evening, strolling around the streets of Paris we were accosted by two very pretty young ladies, who suggested that we may want to sample their wares.

I was not interested, being used to being accosted, and left the two girls alone with Bill and didn't hear what was going on. After a few minutes he left the two girls and caught up to me with a grin on his face, but said nothing.

We eventually landed up in some little bar and later went back to our hotel. I noticed Bill seemed to be keeping an eye on his watch and seemed to be eager to get back to the hotel as soon as possible.

We must have returned about 11:00, and having separate rooms, adjoining to each other, we returned to each his own, and I started to get ready for bed. I hadn't been in bed more than five minutes, when I heard a knock on Bill's door and a female voice saying something when the door opened.

The partition between the two rooms must have been thin, for I could make out and imagine what was going on in Bill's room. But I eventually fell asleep and really didn't give it much thought.

I woke up about 6 a.m. to hear the most awful racket going on in the courtyard under the balcony of Bill's room.

One of the young ladies that we had met on the street was standing in the street, in her bare feet with only a thin dress on, screaming in French up at Bill's room and shaking her fist in obvious rage.

Suddenly Bill appeared on his balcony with clothes and shoes which he threw down at her, and closed his door and went back in.

The poor girl picked up her belongings, still screaming and ranting and left.

When I met Bill for breakfast later in the morning, and we sat down facing each other, I asked what all the noise and ruckus was about with the young lady he had entertained during the night.

Bill looked at me stone faced and said, "What are you talking about, what racket and ruckus, what gives."

I explained what I'd seen and Bill's answer floored me. "I don't know what you are talking about," he said, "You must have been dreaming, or seen somebody else, it certainly wasn't me."

I never pressed the issue, for really it was no business or concern of mine, but I got the feeling that maybe the cost of the night had not been to his liking, and was probably the cause of the argument.

I think that incident was the reason that Bill and I never did see eye to eye on many things and I suppose that I shouldn't be too critical. After all, it was none of my business.

When we first arrived back in America in 1964, we rented an apartment in Fairfield, but we eventually had a house built in Huntington and found it to be a very friendly neighborhood and on our second day there the neighbors arrived at our door step with goodies to bid us welcome. What a difference to Inhurst Woods.

In 1968, Dougie who had joined the U.S. Army was shipped out to Vietnam to fight in that war that was taking place at that time, and to our shock and dismay was mortally wounded and died.

His body was shipped to us by freight train and David and I and the funeral director were down at the freight yard on a cold, drizzly morning to receive his body.

Dooly and I were devastated, after losing little Red in Canada, and now Dougie, we felt lost.

Up to that time, Dooly had never worked, and the doctor who we had at that time, being afraid that Dooly would have a nervous breakdown, suggested that she take up some type of work to help her take her mind off her loss. You can never forget, but time can be a great healer.

Dooly decided to become a nurse, took the L.P.N. course, and I must say it did her a world of good.

She loved nursing, always worked with the elderly in nursing homes, bought herself a little Volkswagon and managed to overcome some of her grief.

While living in Huntington, Eileen who was Dooly's sister had a brother-in-law who was a priest and had been sent to Canada, he came down to visit us and we enjoyed having him for the couple of weeks that he was with us.

I became good friends with Father Jim, and once asked him what made him become a priest, expecting the usual pious answer. He answered quite candidly which surprised me. "I became a priest," he said, "because it was a good living."

He was very eager to stay in the states, for I gathered he didn't care for Canada very much.

In conversations that he had with the local priest in Huntington, I gathered that they would have welcomed him in the church in Huntington and he returned to Canada with the idea of coming back.

Unfortunately, on his return to Canada he fell ill and died. He was such a nice man and it sadden me to think of his death.

I enjoyed working in Bridgeport and made many friends of the people that I worked with.

Phil Sagarin was a Jew, as were his Chief Financial Office, two of his Floor Supervisors, and his Plant Manager and Production Supervisor. But that didn't stop him from promoting me, a Catholic, and making me one of only two Vice Presidents of the company.

I was honored and a little overwhelmed, but unfortunately my promotion was short lived for in 1974, Phil Sagarin sold his company to a large corporation, and in a few short months, I found myself out of a job, for the new company, dismissed most of the managerial staff and brought in their own people.

With the profit sharing that was paid out to me from A.R.C., and a small pension that I received, I felt ready to retire, especially with the profit sharing that I had received and was invested for me in my name, paying me a substantial dividend. But fate was to take a hand and I didn't retire until 10 years later.

When I was laid off at Bridgeport, with the idea of going into some kind of semi retirement, I looked around much of the area, and always being interested in land, I came across a small farm in Thomaston, Connecticut, which suited my purpose well.

Dooly was ecstatic at the idea of me becoming, as she put it, "a tiddly arsed farmer." Where she got that expression from I don't know.

So in 1975, we bought the 40-acre farm, added another 20 acres later and raised polled Herelard cattle, veal, goats and chickens.

One of A.R.C. suppliers of a metal stamping used in the manufacture of our valves was a company in Thomaston and who had been looking for a Quality Control Manager for some time. The man who owned the company Dick Wright, suddenly appeared at my door at the farm, introduced himself, and asked if he could talk to me for a minute.

I let him in the house, and he explained his mission, knew I had been let go at A.R.C., offered me a good salary and would I consider the job.

He said that if I stayed with him for 10 years, he would also guarantee me a good pension.

I explained that if I did take the job, that I would not work for him for 10 years, for I definitely would not work past my 65th birthday.

Being 55-1/2 at that time, I really didn't want the job, although tempted, until he said, you can retire at 65, and I'll give you a pension.

In addition he said that him and his wife had just bought a large R.V. and were going to take a trip around the U.S. in it for a 6-week tour of America.

Dooly was with me, and he suggested we both come on the trip with him and his wife, and my salary would start from that very day, so we would have a 6-week paid vacation, and then start work when we got back.

Needless to say, I took the job. Dooly and I went on a 6-week tour of the states and up into Canada, found his wife to be a charming lady, and the job itself, when I started work, an easy comfortable job right on my door step.

I worked for Dick Wright until I was 65 to the day, retired with a second pension and never regretted it.

When Dougie died, David was devastated by his death for they were inseparable. Dougie, David and Terry. I used to call them the three musketeers. One for all and all for one.

I think David turned to drugs after Dougie died and in 1978, during a visit to Gorey, in Ireland, David died of pneumonia.

In 1968, Terry had returned from England and went to college at the University of Connecticut in Storrs and had graduated in 1972 with a degree in Civil Engineering.

Alanna returned as well, and got an associate degree in Liberal Science.

In 1993, the farm became a little too much for me and we sold it to a man who was from Switzerland who owned a small tool and die company in Thomaston. We then bought a house in Hampton, Connecticut and lived there until 2003.

In 1978, while living on the farm, Rob came out to us and told us he was gay. Although concerned for him, both Dooly and I accepted what he was and it made no difference to our love for him, for he was a good honest lad.

Rob also went to UCONN and graduated in 1984 with a degree in Civil Engineering, the same as Terry.

Again death was to stalk our family, for Rob contracted AIDs and in 1995 he died at home where we had looked after him during the last year of his illness.

He was attending Harvard at the time taking a masters degree in Landscape Design, which was a 3 year course but he failed to finish his final year.

Margie, who was Dooly's sister, lived in Canada with her family and would come down after to see us, and we in turn would visit them occasionally.

Margie on one of our visits, had remarked how many of the Canadians who had immigrated from England, on reaching 65 years of age, were drawing social security from England as well as Canadian pensions.

She remarked, that having served in the military in England and worked for a short time there that I should also be entitled to an English Social Security pension.

She was able to get me a form which I filled out with among other information, my bank account number.

I heard nothing from England for about 3 months, when suddenly one month, on receiving my bank statement, I found a deposit of around $6,000 deposit in it. Back S.S. payments.

In a couple of days later I received a letter from the British S.S. Dept. informing me that my wife and I would in the future be getting a social security check deposited every 28 days in my account. That was in 1985, and at the time of writing this (2009) I have received a check from them every 28 days for the past 24 years.

CHAPTER SIX

As an immigrant who came to this country in 1953, and now when I am 89 years old in 2009, I look back on the years that seem to have gone by so fast, and can't help but compare these United States today to what they were when I first came here.

I am appalled and dismayed, and not a little saddened as I see the terrible destruction and deterioration that has taken place over those 56 years in our society, and in the American way of life.

I still find the average American kind and considerate and I live in a neighborhood where the people around, help me voluntarily in so many ways. Without their help and kindness it would be difficult for me to live alone as I do.

Our economy is in a mess, and with a recession that appears to be headed for a depression that would equal the one in 1930, we look around and ask, who is responsible for all this destruction.

But if we are honest with ourselves, we will look to ourselves for the answer. For we the people, because of our greed in piling up the debts that we have incurred on our credit cards, or houses and cars and it seems on everything we buy, that our financial world has collapsed.

We are encouraged to buy, buy, buy in every advertisement that we see or read on our televisions, newspapers, billboards, and magazines and like pigs at a trough, we hand over our plastic cards in a feeding frenzy. We don't consider whether we can afford it, we have become a people of instant gratification. When the bill comes, we'll pay a minimal amount, and disregard the high interest rates up to 30% in some cases.

But the times come when we have exhausted our line of credit and the financial woes begin.

A larger house we can't afford, a more expensive car to impress our neighbors, they all put us into a debt which we eventually find that we couldn't afford.

The freedom that we fought so hard for in 1760, has become so abused, that the attitude of many people is that we are free to do and act as we wish, regardless of its consequence.

Marriage, which to my way of thinking, is one of the greatest institutions that was ever invented in our society, and it has become a farce.

President Roosevelt revered marriage, and once said and I quote, "As the sanctity of marriage goes, so will the country," and it seems his prophetic words have come true.

Divorce today is so common that it doesn't even make the news. "For better or for worse," means until better comes along.

I mentioned many years ago that I thought that the American males reluctance to accept responsibilities would spill over into his private life. When I see the number of single mothers who wait in vain for that child support check I realize how right I was.

When you see the number of marriages that break apart and the divorce rate today, one out of every two marriages, I shudder to think how the poor children must suffer.

Our government is really no better, and instead of setting an example, our national debt is something over one trillion dollars and growing, and the irony of that debt is a country that politically we despise, China who we borrow from to subsidize our greed.

Our car industry is in a shambles because of incompetence on their part and high wages that the unions demand. Instead of letting them go into bankruptcy and allow them to restructure, our government gives them more billions of our tax dollars which in the long run will do them no good, but put us further into debt.

When I first came to America I worked in a factory and was paid a living wage that enabled me to live a decent life. My wife Dooly never worked an outside job. She had an honorable job as a mother and homemaker, and my wages were sufficient for our needs.

We bought a small but nice home, we had one car, ate well and took nice holidays. Our children went to nice schools, were well dressed and we lived within our means. Credit cards did not exist in those days.

With the average wage of a working man in 2009, it is impossible for him to buy a house, and raise a family without his wife working as well. And this I believe is one of the main causes of the break up of marriage today.

To expect a woman to hold down a full time job, and then to also do the work of being a housewife and mother I think is expecting too much from her.

Take the fact as well that so many Americans shirk the responsibility of marriage, and you have the seeds of disaster.

At one time torture was considered something that was part of the dark ages, and looked on with disgust and horror by numbers of the civilized world.

We have introduced torture as a means of obtaining information from prisoners, and justify our actions with fancy words and rhetoric to fool the public that it is necessary. Nothing justifies torture, and we should consider what will happen to our own soldiers if they are captured and held as prisoners. Would we consider their torture acceptable, tell your answer to the wives and mothers of those soldiers.

The drug scene has taken hold in America, and has given cause to a prison population where one adult in America today out of every 100 adults is incarcerated in our jails. Can you imagine, one out of every 100 adults. It boggles the mind.

Corruption has always to some extent, been a part of the political scene, but in the last few years it has become blatantly common.

To governors of states trying to peddle for there own profit, senate seats, and politicians hiding illegal bribes in refrigerators. To senators who are caught evading income tax illegally, and so many of our leaders and members of our government who are caught with their hands in the cookie jar.

Many of them have been caught and go to jail, but to many of them get away with the illegal acts by employing the smart lawyers who know all the angles to get them off.

Some of our freedoms have been taken away from us by a government that seems to feel it has a right to impose there own interpretation of freedom on the people of this country.

Wire tapping and surveillance has taken from us that right to privacy that we used to hold so dear.

The war that has been going on in Iraq was never condoned by the senate, which it should have been by law. We fight other wars, in Afghanistan and Iraq. With no visible sight of them coming to an end.

Why we ever went to war with Iraq, which has been going on for the last 6 years I'll never know. Our intelligence and surveillance has shown there were no weapons of mass destruction, which was the reason we were given for invading the country in the first place.

Our standing in the eyes of the rest of the world has dropped to record lows.

The present administration is looked on as a bully government and our only hope is that the man who will take over from Bush, will do a better job, but I'm afraid that unless the people of America mend their ways and get behind the new president, we are headed for a real depression.

And maybe when you think of it maybe that wouldn't be so bad, for it would make us all realize that there is a real world out there, and we may be all forced to face up to it and live accordingly.

So when you think of this land of democracy that we have developed, and the fact that we are trying to sell this to a basically Muslim world, it just doesn't make a lot of sense.

Even our churches and our Christian religion has somehow been lost on the way, for they have become places of business, amassing large amounts of wealth which seems contrary to the teachings of Jesus Christ.

It seems to me that instead of trying to impose our way of life on the rest of the world, we should try to understand their point of view, and come to some diplomatic agreements.

But although I write this down with something of a heavy heart, I have not given up hope.

Somehow the goodness that exists in the average American will prevail, but I don't think life will ever be the same again, and that compromising will make us all better people.

We somehow must go back a little in our past, and realize that as long as we have a home, be it ever so humble, that we have food to put on our table, and the love of a family to take care of, all the rest is icing on the cake.

That and the freedoms that were spelled out in the Declaration of Independence are all that we really need, and those are the things we should again strive for.

My journey in this life will soon come to an end, but I end my own history in this journey by thanking God and the Ford Motor Company for giving me the opportunities to live in these United States and to proudly become a citizen.

I doubt if very much of this will ever be read, but I've had the opportunity to put it all down on paper and to be able to remember the 66 years that I have lived in this wonderful land, God Bless America.

Thank you God for giving us humans all the wonderful things that have allowed us to create this wonderful country. May we learn to use them more wisely in the future, than we have done in the past.

CHAPTER SEVEN

But I would like to end this story of my journey through life to a new beginning for me, for gradually I have began to realize that my feeling about God and my relationship to him, have become so different to what I accepted as a Catholic.

To believe in a higher power, who in some way created this whole universe is not a matter of faith, but a logical conclusion.

The universe did not just happen, it must have been created by something, and for want of a better word we call that something God.

When we die, there are only one of two things I believe that can happen to us. One, we have a soul and go on to a new life, we call this Heaven. Two, we have no soul and that is the end of our existence, complete oblivion.

I tend to believe we have a soul and go on to a new 'life.' If God is all powerful, which I believe he is, then I cannot see that he would tolerate the existence of a Devil, let alone allow such a place as Hell to exist.

To God then, there are no such things as good or evil, and our souls when we die return to the universe which we are all a part of.

I think that is the way my God is. Our transgressions on this earth are meaningless to Him. Like weeds they are plucked up and thrown away, discarded and forgotten and God is just happy to see our souls return to Him.

The Ten Commandments which we are told, came from God. I do not believe they came from Him, but are man made. They have become the basis for the laws of our Government and I feel that this is a good thing, for without these laws to govern and control us, life would be chaotic and a shamble (not that it isn't, even with them).

I do not believe in prayer, for He has put on this earth all the things we need for our happiness and wellbeing. It is up to all of us to use those things wisely.

If we want to pray to God, pray only to thank Him, but I don't think He expects it, but it would be a nice thing to do.

Over the years, as humans, we have exploited each other, warred and humiliated, murdered, raped and robbed, and left people so divided in their religious beliefs that one wonders what will be the end of it all for humanity.

My answer is simple, but not an easy one to put in to effect.

We should abandon all your religious myths and fairy tales, teach all children to live by the Golden Rule. Teach them to understand God and His relationship to us. To be appreciative of all that He has given us. And to use those things wisely. Teach them to live on facts, not on fiction. And the fact is that God exists, and how we act as humans affects not only ourselves, but others around us.

Teach them to reach for happiness, for if they have the four basic needs for that happiness when they grow up, they are rich indeed.

A home of their own, be it ever so humble, food to meet their needs, and love in that home that they should cherish. That and to live and teach by the Golden Rule. "To do unto others, as you would have them do unto you."

What I am suggesting is of course, a dream, but it is a dream that has taken its shape in my mind, in part, since my dear wife died.

By the time this gets published, I will be ninety years old, and it is only since I retired that I have time on my hands in which to think, ponder and read, and I feel very confident of the things I have written in this Chapter.

I have partly discussed some of my feelings with a friend of mine who is a retired priest.

One of the answers he had was, that God had given us a free will, a mind to think and act as we wished, to differentiate between good and evil.

If as I think, there is no Devil or Hell, then to God there is no good or evil, and our actions on this earth are really of no concern to Him, and meaningless.

We create laws and rules to govern ourselves, not to satisfy God, and those laws and rules, and the interpretation of what is good or evil, is good to some and the same thing evil to others.

For example, to a Jew to eat pork is evil, to a Christian it is good. To a Muslim for a married woman to go out in public unveiled is evil. To most other religions it is not. Hitler was an evil man in his war against the Jews, killing millions of innocent people. Harry Truman, who was responsible for dropping the atomic bomb on Japan, killing millions of innocent people, was a hero.

So what really is good, and what is evil?

I go back to the Golden Rule, and apply it only to us humans, and take God out of the equation. That rule tells you in itself what is good and what is evil, and if you think about it, it is really the only rule we should live by.

God will not judge us or chide us if we break our own laws and rules, it is up to our peers on this earth to do that. I do not profess to know or understand what Gods plan is for our souls when we die and return to "heaven", or as humans while we live on this earth, but I do know that in the name of religion, be it Judaism, Muslim, Hindu, Christian, or whatever, that religions have been responsible for the creation of so much cruelty and hardship to the human races since the beginning of recorded history and it still continues to this day.

I leave you with one last thought, that religions are, and always have been, instruments of power. We all know that power corrupts and absolute power corrupts absolutely.

EPILOGUE

In 1998, I began to notice that Dooly was becoming very forgetful. She was still the same loving person that she always was, but would forget little things that would happen, and even things of the past.

At first I just dismissed it as aging, for we were both in our 70's, and I felt that it was a normal process of aging that we both would go through.

But as a couple of years past, I began to realize that something was wrong and after taking Dooly to the doctor, and having her examined, she was diagnosed as having Alzheimer's disease.

Her condition gradually worsened as the years went by and there came a time that she didn't really remember who I was, still called me Doug, and still told me that she loved me, I think even more often than she had in the past.

Before the disease took hold, she had always shown me in so many ways how much she loved me and I felt that somehow, in her deteriorating mind, that she felt that she didn't have the same capacity to do the many things that showed her love for me and making up for it in telling me more often that she loved me.

In 2003, she began telling me that she wanted to go home after we came back from Ireland after a two-week holiday with Nial. In December of that year we sold up the house in Hampton and moved in with Nial and stayed for the whole winter until February of 2004. We bought the house I am in now in Dayville, Connecticut a house that was small but suited us in every way.

Dooly was not a hard person to look after, when you love someone as much as I loved Dooly, it comes easy. I don't think Dooly ever realized how sick she was and that she was slowly dieing.

With the help of a wonderful lady, who became a friend that I will never forget, we made Dooly comfortable and happy until the day she died in June of 2007.

When Dooly died I remembered those words written by a poet, "Tis better to have loved and lost than never to have loved at all." And the greatest thing you ever learn, is to love and be loved in return, and I was able to take comfort from them.

I count the blessings that I have left today, the few friends that I have, Margy in Canada who calls me often, and Neal in Ireland who does the same. And Debbie Brown who has helped so much.

And of course, Terry my son, and Alanna my daughter, who I love dearly, and who I am very proud of.

They have both grown into good honest people, and without Terry's help and companionship, it would be very hard for me to live alone as I do.

If I needed her, Alanna would come at the drop of a hat. She is such a good girl, and reminds me a lot of Dooly.

Although I am not as close to my two grandsons as I like, Hunter being far away in Oregon, and Terrence being far away in his own little world. I love them both and say a prayer for them everyday.

NOTES

NOTES

NOTES

NOTES

NOTES

NOTES

www.ingramcontent.com/pod-product-compliance
Lightning Source LLC
Chambersburg PA
CBHW030356290526
45785CB00004B/1780